ART OF SLAP
FOR BASS

Develop Your Own Bass Grooves and Chops Over Various
Slap-Related Styles of Music
By Brian Emmel

T0085623

Brian Emmel can be reached by e-mail at: BEMMEL3694@AOL.com
Brian's newest's CD release are: Johari's Window; & The Invention of Monsters

Special Thanks:
Eric Fuchsman, Frank Green and Working Musician,
Wayne Gard and Gards Music, GHS Strings,
Dale Titus and Bass Frontiers Magazine

Cover art - Eddie Young
Paste-up - Kenneth Warfield
Production - Ron Middlebrook

SAN 683-8022
ISBN 1-57424-053-6

Copyright © 1997 CENTERSTREAM Publishing
P.O. Box 17878 - Anaheim Hills, CA 92817

Table Of Contents

Introduction

How to Use This Book

This book is designed for the advanced beginner to intermediate player.

The main objective to this method of slap is based around the understanding, and application of **MODES**. The focus is on the concept of groove sculpting from the modes, **not** on the actual right and left hand techniques.

In order to benefit from this book you will need to understand **Rhythm Notation**. Tablature is provided for those of you who do not read music notation. I also included a brief glossary of rhythm note and rest values.

This book will most certainly open your mind into the field of options available for you to develop your own bass grooves, and chops over various slap related styles of music.

The CD contains the music for you to:
A) listen to the recorded bass example.
B) observe how it was created.
An explanation of the bass line anatomy is given on the page corresponding to the chart on each following page.
The CD feature allows you to pan the recorded bass line out of the mix and practice crafting your own bass line; simply turn the pan on your CD player to the extreme right.

The box in the left hand column of the page will give the modes that I used to create my bass line or groove over the specific chart on the following page.

The box in the right hand column of the page gives a basic explanation in an anatomical type of outline.

The bottom half of the page was reserved to illustrate the modes in their natural position, where I actually comped my bass parts. The black dots indicate the notes of the modes above and below the tonic. Whether you're a four string, and or five string player, the black dots show the position boundaries to experiment with your own improvisational bass lines.

The Circle of Fifths

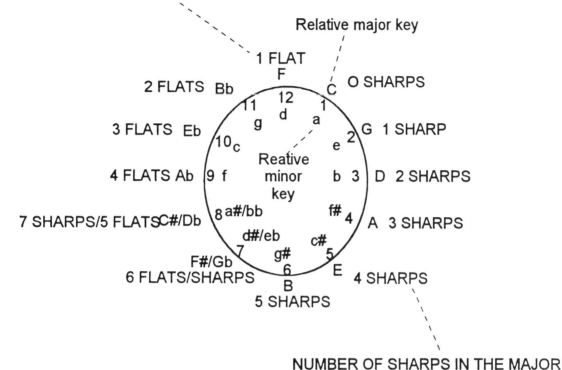

NUMBER OF FLATS IN THE MAJOR KEY

Relative major key

1 FLAT F

O SHARPS

2 FLATS Bb

3 FLATS Eb

G 1 SHARP

4 FLATS Ab

Reative minor key

D 2 SHARPS

7 SHARPS/5 FLATS C#/Db

A 3 SHARPS

F#/Gb
6 FLATS/SHARPS

E 4 SHARPS

5 SHARPS

NUMBER OF SHARPS IN THE MAJOR

The Best way to practice. The circle of fifths starts with the key of C. The musical alphabet in this key contains no sharps or flats. The next key will be G, which is five degrees above the key of C. The seventh of each scale is sharped. Therefore, the seventh tone form G in the G scale is F#. The next key is D major. The seventh tone in the D scale is a C#; so we carry over the F# from the G scale, and add it with the C# (seventh in D). Remember to always carry over the previous sharps to the next key in the circle of fifths. This is the only difference between each scale or key. Every time we go up to the next key, we will add a sharp to the seventh degree.

The Musical Alphabet makes it easy to learn the notes contained in each key. A B C D E F G, are the seven natural notes contained in the key of C major (all the white keys on a piano). These seven notes also become **Tonics** for seven of twelve keys of music. The remaining five notes: A#/Bb C#/Db D#/Eb F#/Gb G#/Ab (all the black keys on the piano), are also known as **Enharmonics** until they are placed into their natural scale or keys.

Knowledge of all twelve keys helps one to understand modes, and their function in the keys. I recommend starting with the key of C major, and working clockwise in the circle.

Definition of Scale Degrees

**Scales and modes are constructed from half and whole step interval combinations.
This illustration uses the C major key as a global example.**

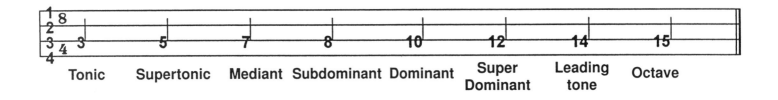

Tonic   Supertonic   Mediant   Subdominant   Dominant   Super Dominant   Leading tone   Octave

Tonic: means tone, which in turn indicates the main tone or root tone of the scale.

Supertonic: super is a prefix meaning "above". Therefore supertonic indicates the tone above the tone, or the tone above the tonic.

Mediant: refers to the third, E, which derives from the tonic triad C-E-G which constructs a C major chord. Mediant means middle or center.

Subdominant: means the dominant below the dominant. It's harmonic function is valued a little less than the dominant in major and minor keys.

Dominant: because of it's harmonic omnipotence in major and minor keys. It is also known as the key center.

Super Dominant: Dominant "above" the dominant, the sixth degree also can change the major key to it's relative minor key, which introduces a whole new harmonic scale structure. The harmonic minor scale.

Leading Tone: the word "leading" implying an impending resolution to the octave.

Octave: oct-meaning eight, this is the eighth tone of the scale, same tone as the tonic.

CD Track list:

1, Beginning Monologue
2, Tuning
3, Einstein's Song
4, Frank & Stein
5, Fro Lik
6, Danger in the Undertow
7, Rap it Up
8, Rap it Up 2
9, Funky Brewster
10, Emma's Dilemma
11, Dali's Llama
12, House 4 Sale
13, House Party
14, Genitourinary Man
15, Beheaded Chicken Dance
16, Ending Monologue

Modes

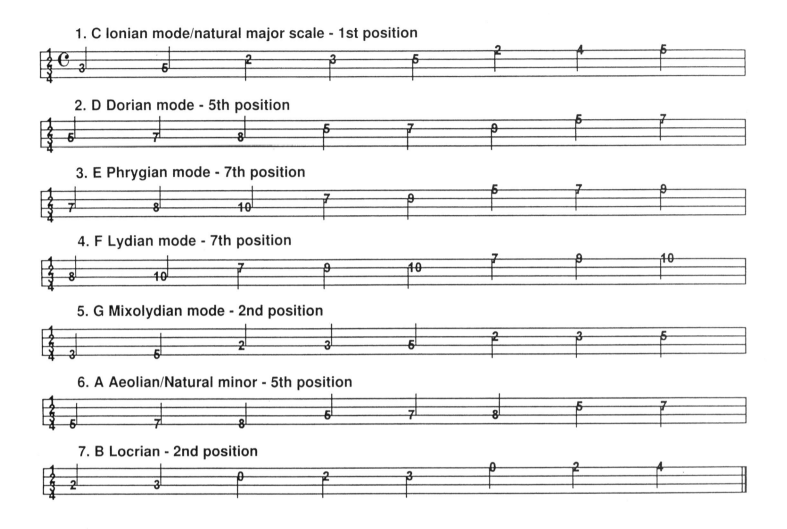

1. C Ionian mode/natural major scale - 1st position

2. D Dorian mode - 5th position

3. E Phrygian mode - 7th position

4. F Lydian mode - 7th position

5. G Mixolydian mode - 2nd position

6. A Aeolian/Natural minor - 5th position

7. B Locrian - 2nd position

Positions are marked by indicating the placement of the 1st or index finger

The above examples of the seven modes are illustrated in the key of C major.
A mode is merely a scale beginning on various degrees, or intervals within the major scale, also known as the Ionian mode.
One should practice playing the modes from each scale degree of the major scale:
**Tonic/Ionian
Supertonic/Dorian
Mediant/Phrygian
Subdominant/Lydian
Dominant/Mixolydian
Superdominant/Aeolian
Leading Tone/Locrian**

Ascend to it's octave, and descend back to it's root tone.

Concentrate on it's sound or melodic content. This is great ear training. This allows one to learn the effects each mode has when played over a specific piece of music.
Finally, practice the modes in all twelve major keys.
See *The Circle of Fifths"*.

Einstein's Song

The Modes And Keys Used:

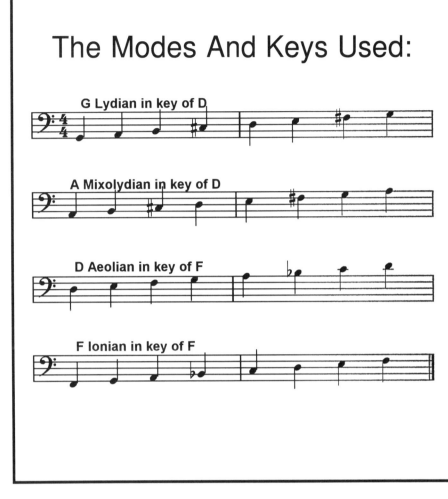

G Lydian in key of D

A Mixolydian in key of D

D Aeolian in key of F

F Ionian in key of F

The Art of The Slap:

The bass lines on this chart are crafted from modal substitutions. Substitutions in this application merely means that we use a different tone arrangement other than the fundamental arrangement over the chord changes. For example: A7sus, belongs to the key of D, which we'd primarily use the A Mixolydian mode to comp our bass line; instead we sub the A Mixolydian arrangement for the G Lydian modal arrangement; which also belongs to the key of D, to comp our bass line.

Over the Dm7/11 we'll use both, the fundamental mode of D Aeolian and F Ionian over the last eight bars; both modes belonging to the key of F.

G Lydian

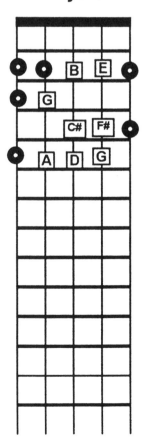

A Mixolydian

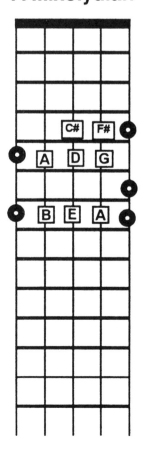

D Aeolian

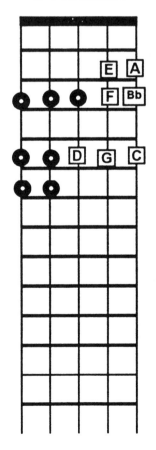

F Ionian

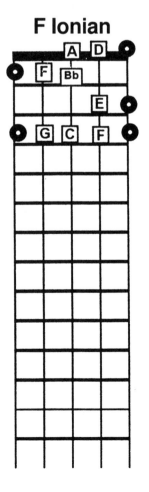

Einstein's Song

Frank & Stein

The Modes And Keys Used:

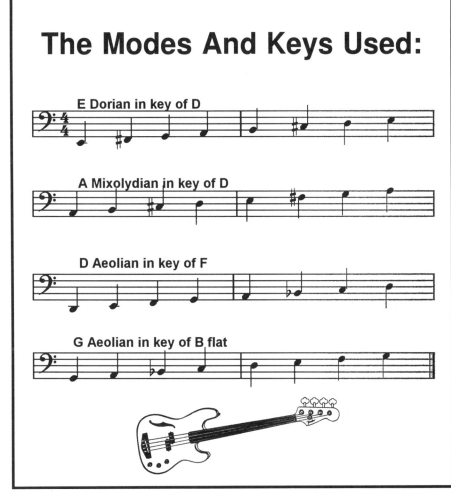

E Dorian in key of D

A Mixolydian in key of D

D Aeolian in key of F

G Aeolian in key of B flat

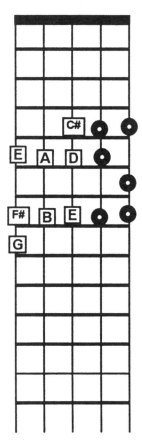

The Art of The Slap:

The bass lines on this chart are crafted from modal substitutions. Substitutions in this application merely means that we use a different tone arrangement other than the fundamental arrangement over the chord changes. For example: A7sus, belongs to the key of D, which we'd primarily use the A Mixolydian mode to comp our bass line; instead we sub the A Mixolydian arrangement for the E Dorian modal arrangement; which also belongs to the key of D, to comp our bass line.

Over the Dm7/11 we'll use the fundamental mode of D Aeolian and exchange G Aeolian over the same Dm7/11 chord; here we use the cross modulation method from fundamental key of F to the sub key of Bb.

E Dorian   **A Mixolydian**   **G Aeolian**   **D Aeolian**

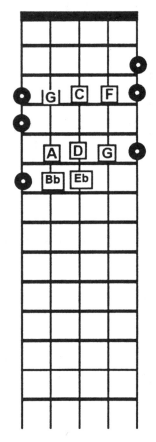
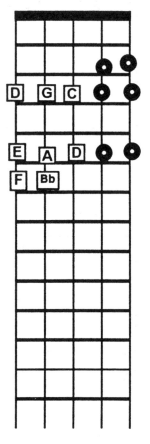

Frank & Stein

(This one's a monster)

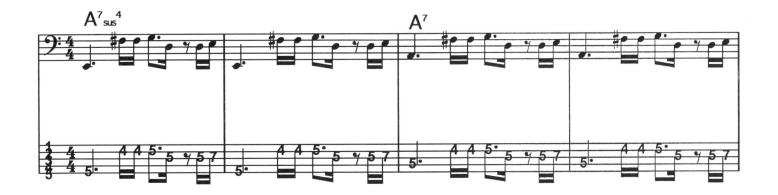

9

Fro Lik

The Modes And Keys Used:

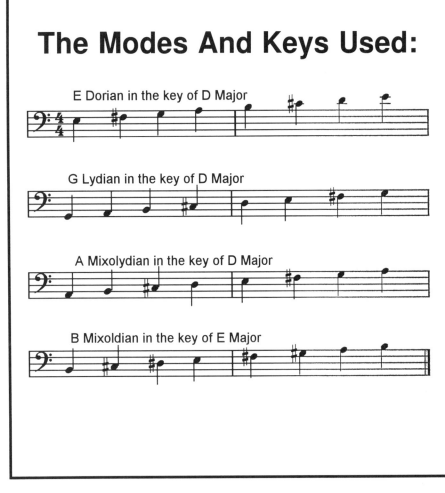

E Dorian in the key of D Major

G Lydian in the key of D Major

A Mixolydian in the key of D Major

B Mixoldian in the key of E Major

The Art Of The Slap:

Fro-Lik is a disco chart. The bass lines are crafted from traditional disco licks, which incorporate alot of root and perfect eight intervals, A.K.A. (octaves).

The groove is usually eighth note rhythms, and is played with staccato, or quick released notes.

Although the style is primarily octave playing, the E Dorian mode can be used to spice up the groove, suggested for fills. Also, the E Aeolian mode, which is the E Natural minor scale can be applied.

A Mixolydian coming out of the key of D can be used over the A and G chords. And B Mixolydian over the B7 chord transition into the song pick-up at bar eight.

E Dorian

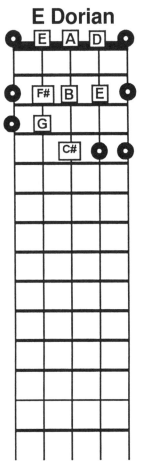

G Lydian

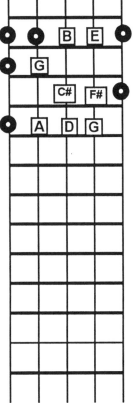

A Mixolydian

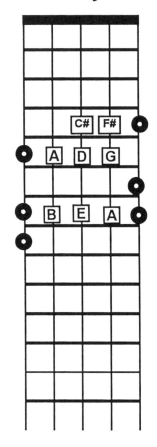

B Mixolydian

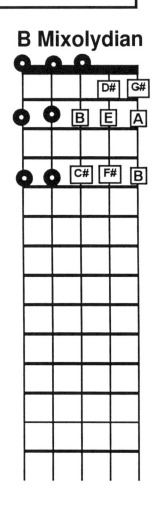

Fro Lik

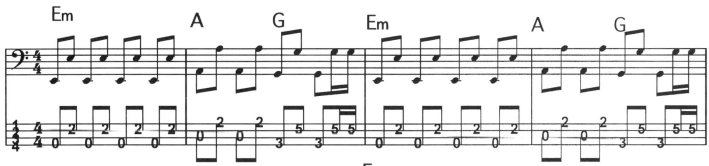

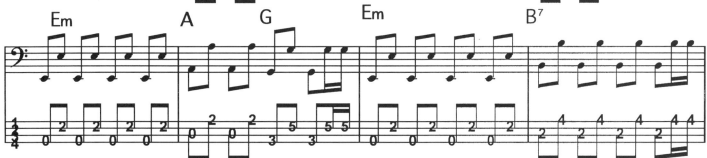

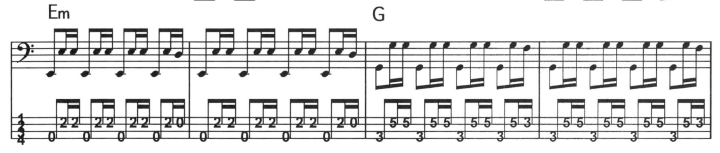

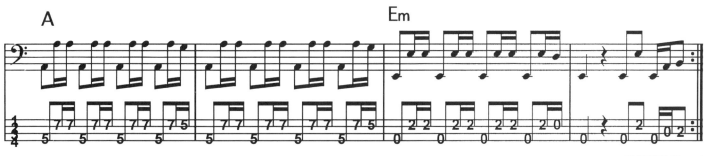

The Modes And Keys Used:

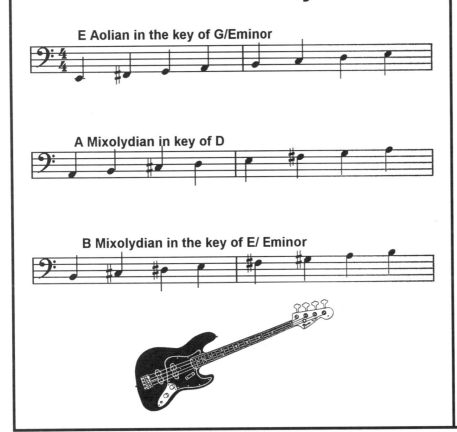

E Aolian in the key of G/Eminor

A Mixolydian in key of D

B Mixolydian in the key of E/ Eminor

The Art of The Slap:

This is a great example of how the modes can be used to develop a simple melodic bass line.

The chart is based in the key of E minor, the B7 chord in the key of E actually acts as a secondary dominant chord; although it can be observed as the five chord in the key of E minor, which is relative to the key of G.

In bars 9-11, we have a "false modulation," or a chromatic movement from the Dma7/9 to the Dbm7 to the Cma7 to the B7. The B7 is also the five chord to the one chord in E minor.

I also intended this arrangement to be played from open position, to practice on open note control.

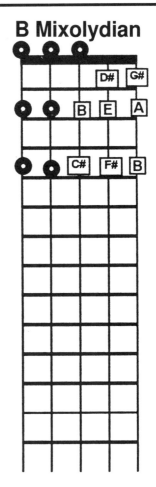

E Aeolian	A Mixolydian	B Mixolydian

Danger In The Undertow

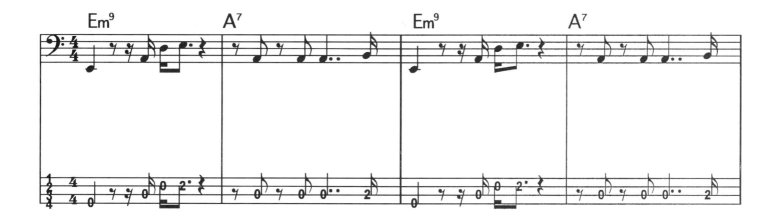

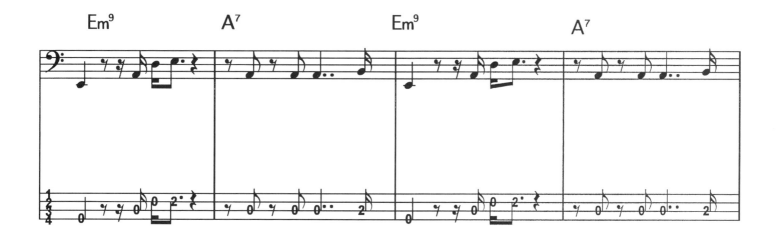

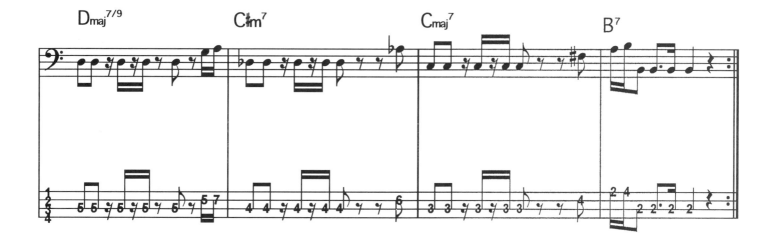

13

Rap It Up

The Modes And Keys Used:

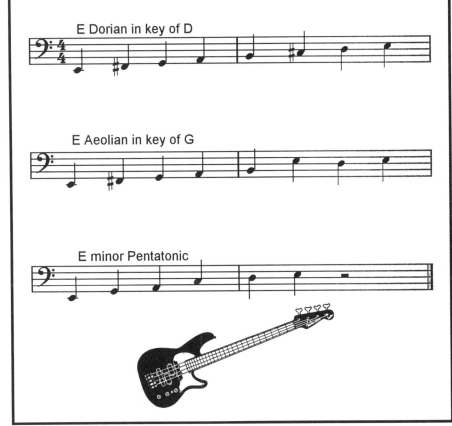

E Dorian in key of D

E Aeolian in key of G

E minor Pentatonic

The Art of The Slap:

"Rap it Up" (1st version) works on the thumb technique. Short note enunciation with the kick drum. This exercise also helps development of open note control muting on the fourth, open E string. Once the thumb locks in tight with the bass drum, experiment with bringing in licks from the E Dorian, and E minor Pentatonic scales for additive flavor over the E minor chord. This exercise also introduces slap and pop techniques over two adjacent strings, (E and A strings).

"Rap it Up 2"
Bars nine through sixteen employ the E Natural minor or Aeolian scale. Notice, also, the descending arpeggio licks. Experiment interchanging the modes.

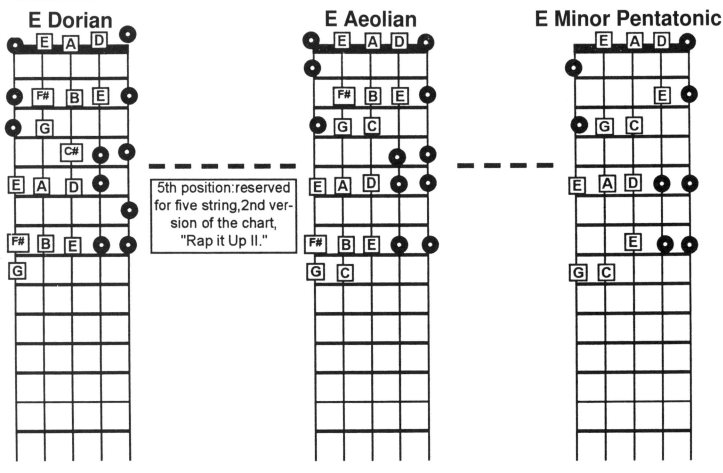

E Dorian

E Aeolian

E Minor Pentatonic

5th position: reserved for five string, 2nd version of the chart, "Rap it Up II."

Rap It Up

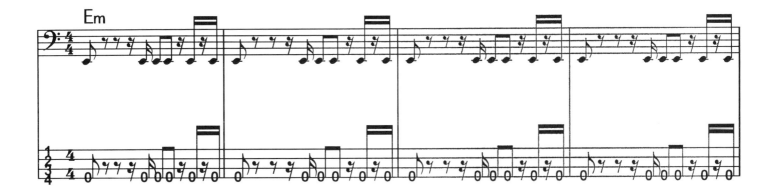

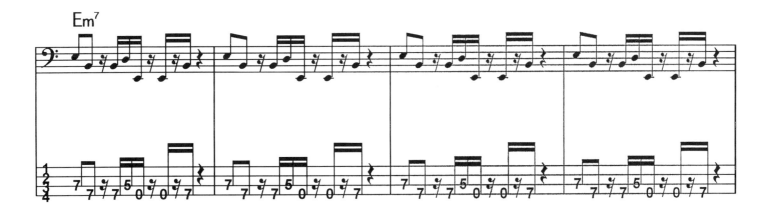

Rap It Up 2

Funky Brewster

The Modes And Keys Used:

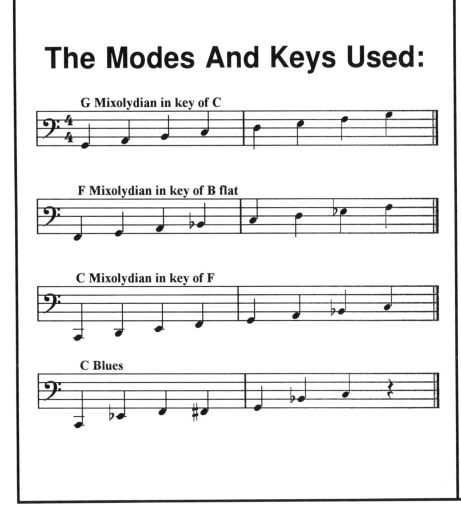

G Mixolydian in key of C

F Mixolydian in key of B flat

C Mixolydian in key of F

C Blues

The Art of The Slap:

These bass lines are crafted from the Mixolydian modes; the Mixolydian mode starts on the 5th scale tone in the Natural Major scale. I prefer to call modes, Tone Centers <u>in</u> the Major scale.

The chart on the next page involves 3 keys of music: The keys are C(G7), F(C7), and B flat(F7). Another way to view this chart is a I-IV-V Blues progression in the key of C Blues; thus using the C Blues scale to comp your bass line.

The tone centers below are spelled out for you, but feel free to improvise with scale tones outside of the highlighted areas (notes above and below the Tone Center or Mode).

G Mixolydian

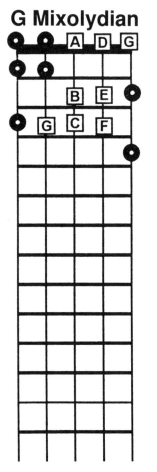

C Mixolydian

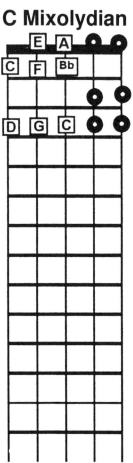

C Blues

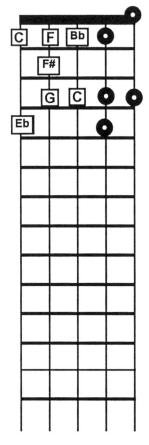

F Mixolydian

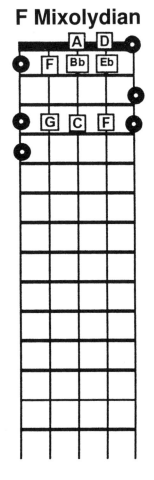

Funky Brewster

19

Emma's Dilemma

The Modes And Keys Used:

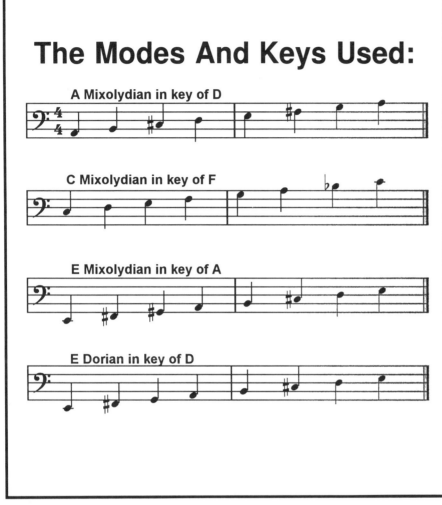

A Mixolydian in key of D

C Mixolydian in key of F

E Mixolydian in key of A

E Dorian in key of D

The Art of The Slap:

The bass lines to "Emma's Dilemma" is crafted from the Mixolydian modes, the Mixolydian mode starts on the 5th scale tone in the Natural Major scale. I prefer to call modes, Tone Centers in the Major scale.

The E Dorian mode comes off the second degree of the D Major scale, and can be used to sub for the E Mixolydian mode, played over the E7 chord.

This chart is composed of all key center, or dominant chord types. The A7 and A7/9 is the key center for the key of D, the C7 for the key of F and the E7 for the key of A.

A Mixolydian   **C Mixolydian**   **E Mixolydian**   **E Dorian**

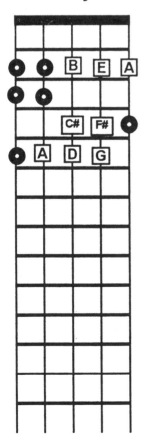 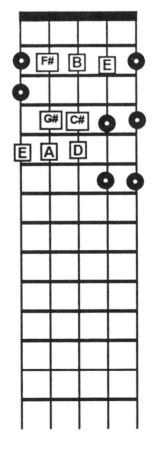 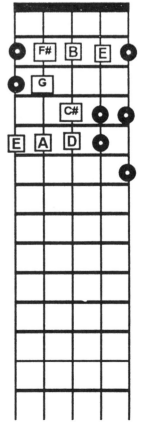

Emma's Dilemma

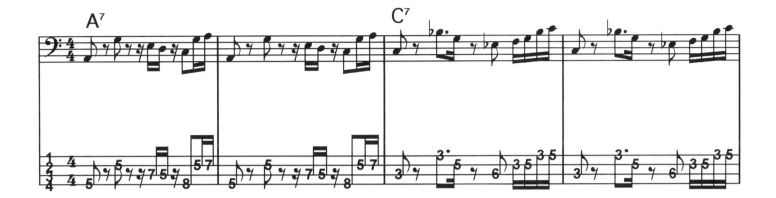

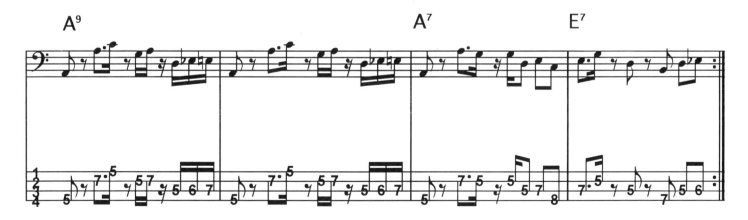

Dali's Llama

The Modes And Keys Used:

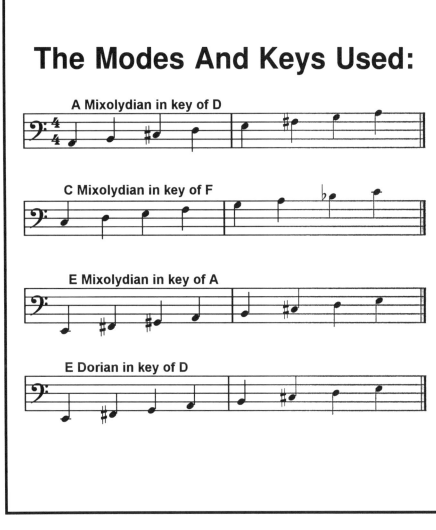

A Mixolydian in key of D

C Mixolydian in key of F

E Mixolydian in key of A

E Dorian in key of D

The Art of The Slap:

The bass lines to "Dali's Llama" is crafted from the Mixolydian mode. The Mixolydian mode starts on the 5th scale tone in the Natural Major scale.

The E Dorian mode comes off the second degree of the D Major scale, and can be used to sub for the E Mixolydian mode, played over the E7 chord.

The chart on the next page involves 3 keys of music: the keys are D(A7 chord belongs), F(C7 chord) and A(E7 chord).

The tone centers below are spelled out for you, but feel free to improvise with scale tones outside of the highlightd areas (notes above and below the Tone Center or Mode).

A Mixolydian

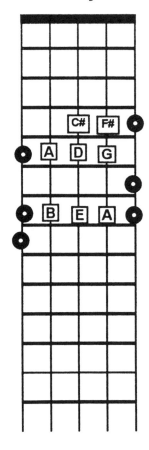

C Mixolydian

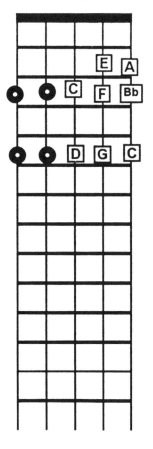

E Mixolydian

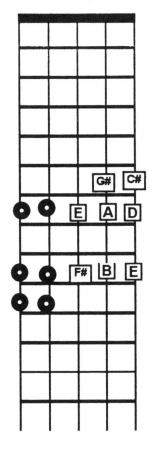

E Dorian

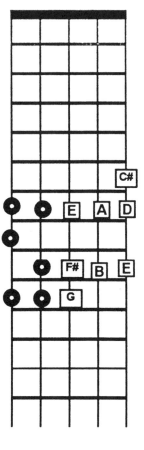

22

Dali's Llama

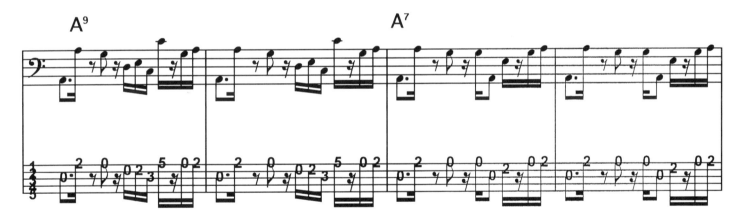

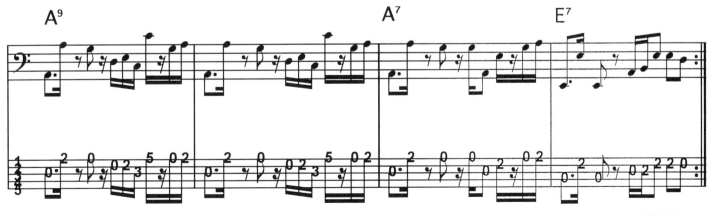

The Modes And Keys Used:

The Art of The Slap:

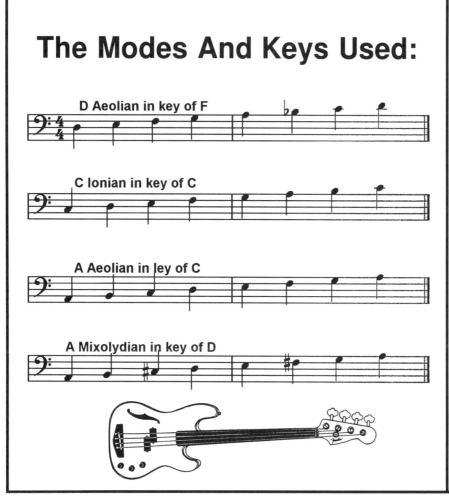

"House 4 Sale" employs the D Aeolian mode from the key of F, C Ionian mode from the key of C, A Aeolian mode from the key of C, and the A Mixolydian mode from the key of D.

The A7 also belongs to the key of D minor, coming out of it's Harmonic minor scale, relative to the F Major scale.

Over the Dm7 chords, I used the D Aeolian modes to comp my bass lines.

Over the Am7 in bar 5, I substituted the C Ionian mode in place of a pure minor, or Aeolian mode.

I then used the A Aeolian mode over bars 13-15, and the A Mixolydian in the final 16th bar.

D Aeolian	C Ionian	A Aeolian	A Mixolydian

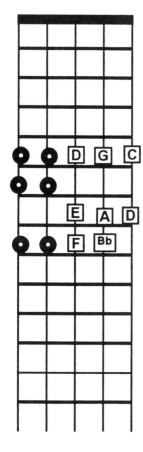
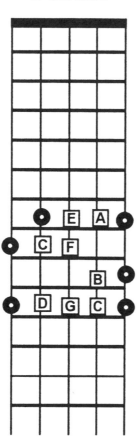
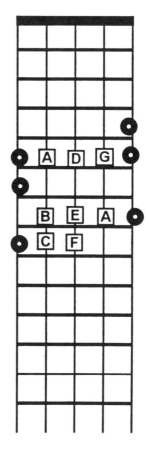
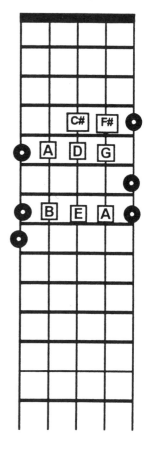

House 4 Sale

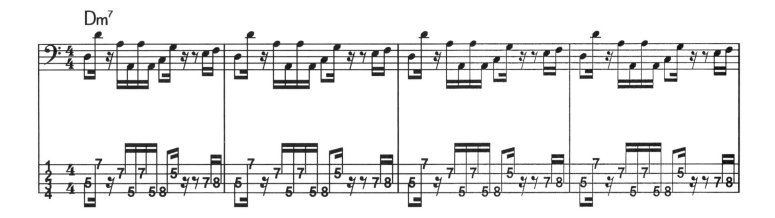

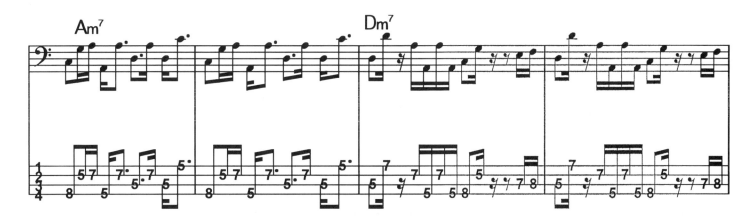

The Modes And Keys Used:

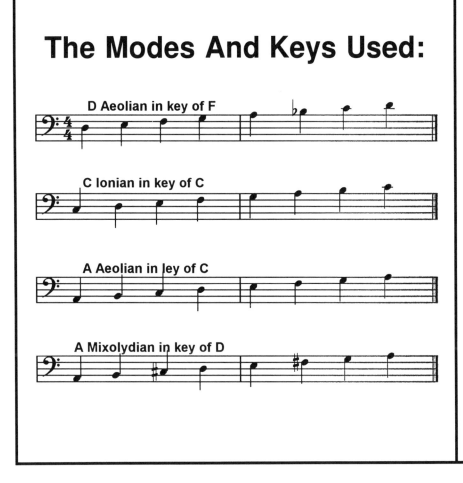

D Aeolian in key of F

C Ionian in key of C

A Aeolian in key of C

A Mixolydian in key of D

The Art of The Slap:

"House Party" employs the D Aeolian mode from the key of F, A Aeolian mode from the key of C and the A Mixolydian mode from the key of D.

The A7 also belongs to the key of D minor, coming out of it's Harmonic minor scale, relative to the F Major scale.

Over the Dm7 chords, I used the D Aeolian modes to comp my bass lines. I then used the A Aeolian mode over bars 5, 6, 13-15, and the A Mixolydian in the final 16th bar.

D Aeolian

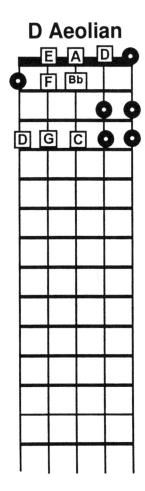

A Aeolian

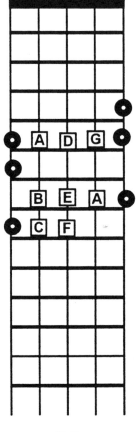

A Mixolydian

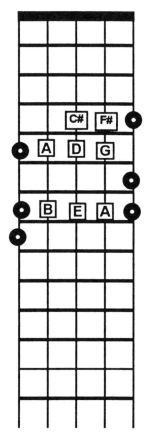

House Party

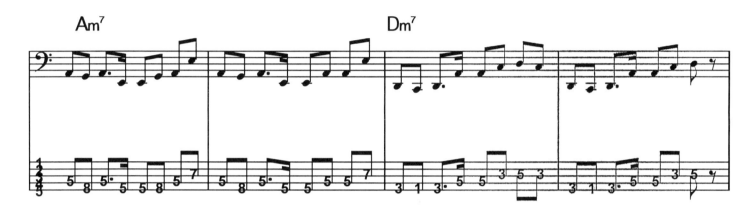

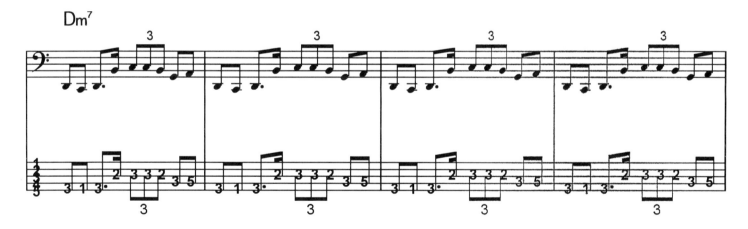

27

Genitourinary Man

The Modes And Keys Used:

E Aeolian in key of G

A Dorian in key of G

B Mixolydian in key E

G Ionian in key of G

F Lydian in key of C

The Art of The Slap:

The chart on the following page contains a couple key changes. The groove is very modal. This is a great example of how the modes can be used to develop a simple molodic bass line.

The E Aeolian mode will play over the Em7 chord. The A Dorian over the Am7 chord. The B Mixolydian over the B7 chord. The G Ionian works over the Gma7/9, and F Lydian works over the Fma7/9.

The chart is based in the key of G, the B7 chord in the key of E actually acts as a secondary dominant chord, although it can be observed as the five chord in the key of E minor, which is relative to the key of G.

E Aeolian

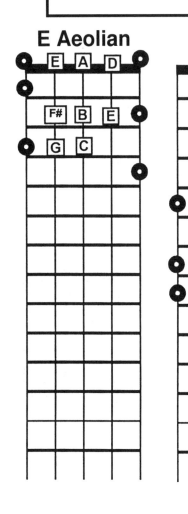

A Dorian

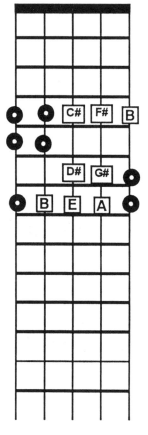

B Mixolydian

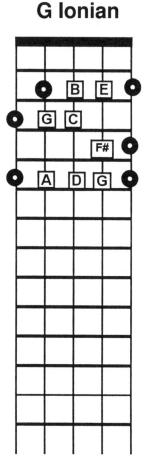

G Ionian

F Lydian

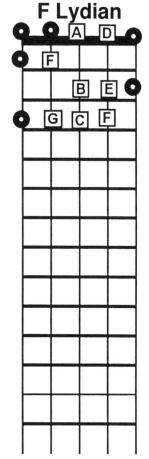

Genitourinary Man

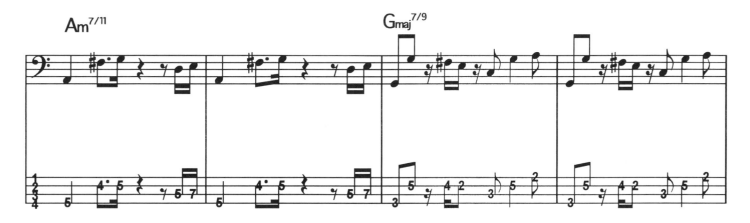

Beheaded Chicken Dance

The Modes And Keys Used:

A Aeolian in the key of A minor

G Mixolydian in the key of C

F Lydian in the key of C

E Mixolydian in the key of A minor

The Art of The Slap:

The chart on the next page contains bass lines sculpted out of two keys: the key of A minor, relative to C major, and the key of F minor, relative to the key of Ab major.

The E7 chord naturally belongs to the key of A major, but in this case it is coming from the key of A minor. The E7 chord is built from the A Harmonic minor scale too.

The A Aeolian mode is used over the Ami7, Ami7/11 chords. The F Aeolian mode is used over the Fmi7, Fmi7/11 chords. The G Mixolydian mode plays over the G chord and the E Mixolydian mode over the E7sus, E7 chords.

A Aeolian

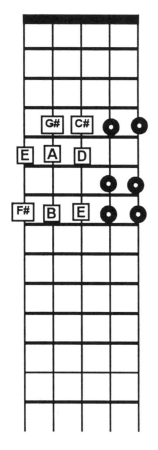

G Mixolydian

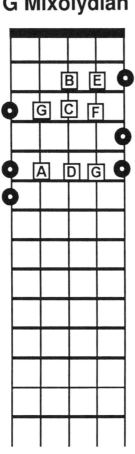

F Lydian

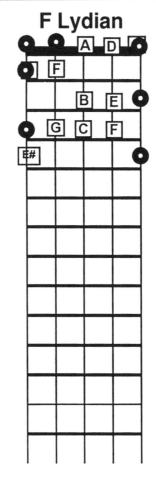

E Mixolydian

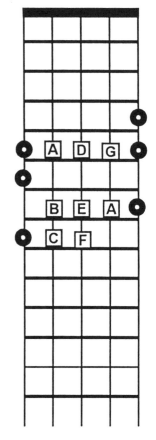

Beheaded Chicken Dance

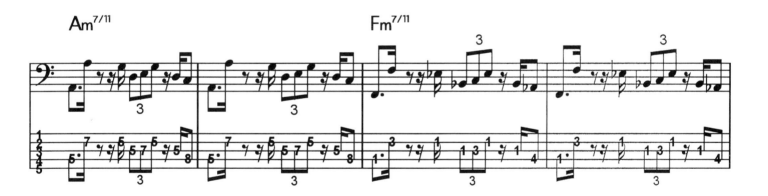

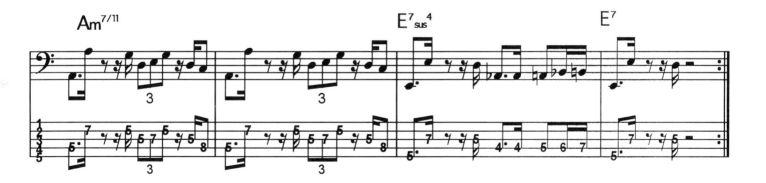

31

Bass books from Centerstream Publishing

P.O. Box 17878 - Anaheim Hills, CA 92807 - P/F (714) - 779-9390
Email: Centerstrm@AOL.com

- Brian Emmel Bass Books -

SCALES AND MODES FOR THE 5-STRING BASS

by Brian Emmel
foreword by Mark Egan
Centerstream Publications
The most comprehensive and complete scale book written especially for the 5-string-bass. Divided into 4 main sections: 1) Scale Terminology 2) Scales 3) Fingerboard chart and diatonic triads 4) Scale to Chord Guide – tying it all together and showing what scale to use over various chords.
_____00000146..............................$9.95

ROCKIN' CHRISTMAS FOR 5-STRING BASS

by Brian Emmel
Centerstream Publications
12 of the most popular Christmas songs arranged for rock guitar, including sweep picking and two-hand tapping, and cool string bending. Songs include: What Child Is This? • Joy To The World • Silent Night • We Wish You A Merry Christmas • and more. Correlates with *Rockin' Christmas For Guitar.*
_____00000172..............................$9.95

BASS GUITAR CHORDS

Centerstream Publications
84 of the most popular chords for bass guitar, including: finger placement, note construction, chromatic charts and most commonly used bass scales. Also has helpful explanation of common 2-5-1 progression, and the chords in all keys.
_____00000073..............................$2.95

Art of the Slap*

This slap bass method book, designed for advanced beginning to intermediate bassists, is based on the understanding and application of modes. The focus in on the concept of groove sculpting from modes, and not on actual right and left hand techniques. The CD features recordings of all the examples, plus a split-channel option to let you practice your playing. Includes 13 songs.
00000229 Book/CD Pack $19.95

5-STRING BASS METHOD

by Brian Emmel
Centerstream Publications
The 5-string bass is rapidly growing into the future and this is your handbook to meet it there. Besides discussing how to adapt to the differences in the 5-string versus 4-, this book explores the various ways of using the 5-string, practice tips, different techniques, and practical applications to various genres demonstrated through songs on the 37-minute accompanying cassette.
_____00000134 Book/Cassette Pack $15.95

5-STRING BASSIC FUNDAMENTALS – THE FUN APPROACH TO BASS IMPROVISATION

by Brian Emmel
Centerstream Publications
This fun new bass method will help you improve your solos, grooves, and bass lines, no matter what style you play. Accompanying CD includes recorded examples.
_____00000086 Book/CD Pack $17.95

CREATING RHYTHM STYLES FOR 5-STRING BASS WITH DRUM ACCOMPANIMENT

by Brian Emmel
Centerstream Publications
This book is designed for bassists to program the written drum grooves into a drum machine and develop a working knowledge over the rhythms and various styles. Drummers can play the written patterns along with a bassist and both can elaborate their playing skills over each examples. The accompaniment CD allows you to fade out the bass guitar part on the left channel or the drums on the right channel.
_____00000162 Book/CD Pack $17.95

PURRFECT 4-STRING BASS METHOD

by Brian Emmel
Centerstream Publishing
This book will teach students how to sight read and to acquire a musical vocabulary. Includes progressive exercises on rhythm notation, 1st to 4th string studies, enharmonic studies, chords and arpeggios, blues progressions and chord charts.
_____00000201..............................$9.95

. . .I'm here to proclaim that this is one of the best books ANY beginner, regardless of age will find today. . .I recommend this book to teachers who have sought but not found a great book to start their beginners off with. . .--Jim Hyatt, BASS Frontiers Magazine

Video

Beginning 5-String Bass

by Brian Emmel
This hour-long video is all you'll need to build a lasting foundation on the 5-string bass! Brian will take you through all the basic techniques, with exercises to help you develop familiarity on the 5-string. Includes information on scale patterns, how to practice, chords and chord substitution, slap technique, and rhythm patterns such as rock, R&B, shuffle, country, soul, funk, and blues. All exercises and patterns are shown in standard notation and tablature in the 18-page booklet that comes with the video. 60 minutes.
00000199 . . . . $19.95

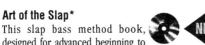